GET-REAL
MINDSET

GET-REAL MINDSET

A Practical Approach To Winning At The Margin

HARRY S. CAMPBELL

With great thanks to the hundreds of friends and

family members who have supported *Team Kris Campbell*

as a part of the *Head for the Cure Foundation*

and our efforts to find a cure for brain tumors.

You bless us.

Proceeds

100% of Harry's *Get-Real* speaking fees and proceeds from book sales benefit the *Head for the Cure Foundation*. His *Get-Real* donations exceeded $400,000 in November 2019.

In October 2003, Harry and his wife Kris registered for the inaugural *Head for the Cure* 5K to support their friend, Matt Anthony, who had lost his brother, Chris, to a brain tumor earlier that year. Neither suspected brain cancer would affect their immediate family just four months later.

Kris was diagnosed in February 2004, at age 34, with a grade II astrocytoma brain tumor. Although her tumor has been slow-growing, it is a malignant form of brain cancer and has proved to be inoperable.

The Campbells, along with their family and friends, have funneled their fundraising and awareness efforts into the *Head for the Cure* through "Team Kris Campbell." Consistently a top team in fundraising and participation, "Team Kris Campbell" has raised over $450,000 since 2004 and recruits 150 to 200 walkers, runners and strollers for the annual *Head for the Cure – Metro KC* 5K.

www.headforthecure.org/teamkriscampbell

About *Head for the Cure*

The *Head for the Cure Foundation* is a 501(c)(3) nonprofit organization dedicated to raising awareness and funding in the fight against brain cancer.

Head for the Cure is committed to providing ongoing financial support to programs including the Brain Tumor Trials Collaborative (BTTC), a network of NCI-accredited medical centers with the expertise and the desire to participate in state-of-the-art clinical trials investigating new treatments for malignant brain tumors.

***Team Kris Campbell,* Head for the Cure 2017**

(Photo credit: Nan Grube)

Contents

Author's Note

One thing should be clear: I'm not a success expert – if such a thing exists! I'm average – in athletic ability, family background, financial roots and looks. You almost assuredly wouldn't pick me as "Most Likely" anything.

But I have been successful in business. I started in marketing at Procter & Gamble (P&G) and performed well enough to be assigned to a newly created, multi-functional team pioneering a unique relationship with Walmart.

While I was in Northwest Arkansas for P&G working with Walmart, Sam Walton infused into me some of his secrets for success that breed results, relationships and respect – and I embraced them wholeheartedly.

After P&G, I headed to a leadership role at the telecom Sprint, then from there to an energizing stint as co-owner of MAI, an award-winning small sports marketing agency. Then it was on to an internet start-up called *uclick*. After the start-up failed to get the traction needed to succeed, I came back to Sprint, then on to a wire line telecom spin-off known as Embarq, and from there to become CEO of a refractive eye surgery company.

(A friend who heard this litany of work settings asked dryly, "What is it? You have trouble holding down a job?" I could see his point.)

But in my view, I had jumped into new roles and produced in settings with new challenges. I was presented with a raft of opportunities to learn while working at and leading companies of ALL sizes. Then once I accomplished what I'd set out to do, my interests changed or the company's situation changed, I'd move on to the next challenge.

In many of the situations I found myself in, I was not favored to come out a winner. I was often the underdog. Either I didn't know the industry I was entering, or the scope of the responsibility was larger than I'd ever experienced before, or the resources at hand didn't seem to be a fit for what we needed to produce. Yet my career trajectory had moved steadily upward – in responsibility, visibility and profitability.

Winning at the Margin

We often think winning happens by crushing it. However, I've built a success strategy not on the power of wide-margin victories, but on the focus of flipping the close losses to wins.

When the margin for error is narrow, the win-loss determination often happens while the ball is in the air. Though you might be the slight underdog, you are able to flip the close losses or win the toss-ups.

I don't win every time; there are always situations in which I'm so outclassed in intellect, experience, resources, etc. But I've found in life that these are actually rarer than you'd think. More often, the question of who wins is determined not by an avalanche, but by a slim margin.

Through my life I've been scouting the horizon – studying leaders, research and my own experience – to find that small strategy that could help me win the close calls.

I have concluded that having a *Get-Real* mindset really matters. This means focusing on the three approaches I have outlined – be an attractor, embrace crookedness and live to learn – in an effort to win more of the toss-ups and flip many of the close losses.

Stated another way, the *Get-Real* mindset uncovers the "extra" intangible needed for winning at the margin!

Prologue

Getting the "Mindset" Ball Rolling

The email asking me to present a kick-off speech for a business conference didn't surprise me; I'd done this many times. But my pause came when I understood what I had actually been invited to do.

An organization was hosting a Start-up Weekend at a local university in the Kansas City area. It wouldn't be just a bunch of curiosity-seekers gathered to hear theories about how to make a business start-up successful.

Rather, in the time allocated to the conference (over the weekend!), the entrepreneurs attending would be immersed in an actual experience of start-up creation, complete with final presentations before the evaluators. And the "winners" would be well positioned to catch the eye of potential investors.

There would be no dull-eyed, text-checking sideliners in this crowd. They'd be doers and aspiring entrepreneurs who were likely taking time off from their bill-paying day job for a shot at going after their personal dreams.

And they'd be gutsy, because by signing up for this weekend, they had chosen a setting where they'd have to be insightful and productive, not just trade baloney about all the things they pretended to know.

My kind of people! They were coming seeking success and committed to scramble for it. My job, as kick-off speaker, was to give them something as real and gutsy as they were to help move them toward that success.

Increase your odds of winning

What I offered them had to be *proven*, that I knew for sure. These listeners hadn't come to see a bunch of Successories memes pulled from the Internet. Just like the ideas they were going to pitch, my success strategies had to have been tested and shown effective.

The ideas had to be *practical*. This crowd included young and older, minimum wage earners and higher-money tech types, some producers and sellers of completely new inventions and others who were upgrading older ones, and a bunch of idea-generating companies stuck between. If the success ideas applied to only some of them, I'd waste the time of everyone else. And I didn't see these folks given to time-wasting.

The ideas also had to be *pared down*. Most of these were people already working a job or two, and some had a kid or three, and too many life obligations to juggle. They wouldn't hold onto 22 secrets to *anything*, even if the payoff to implementing all 22 appeared huge.

I knew a vast percentage of start-ups fail, so the stakes were very high.

That's why anything I told them had to be *real*. *"Get Real"* is a life mantra for me; it's the way I evaluate business leadership behaviors and culture-change strategies. Are they authentic approaches? Do they "smell" true and honest, and promote truth and honesty in others? Whatever I spoke about absolutely had to adhere to the *Get-Real* standard.

What would matter to these entrepreneurial folks?

Wow. I felt the weight of this one. It's one thing to inspire or challenge a room full of people who have solid salaries but want to do a little better. It's another to advise those who are close to jumping off the Cliff of the Great Idea, some of them risking savings, and career tracks and security to make the giant leap.

What did I wish I had known that would have made work in all these settings I'd inhabited easier? And what would have increased my chances of success? What seemed to have increased chances of success for the standouts among the thousands who had worked for me and with me?

For this Start-up Weekend speech, I needed to define what I believed helped make these successes happen for a pretty ordinary guy from rural southern Indiana.

One thing I knew: I'd better narrow the ideas to personal qualities, not specific to any business or professional roles, since the audience represented a bucket load of various businesses and an equally large number of roles, from leader of a good-sized team to a solo business operator working from her basement. I needed to reach all of these folks!

Once I thought about personal success and those who were achieving it, three focus areas surfaced – relationships, resilience and renewal – with a specific winning approach associated with each.

- Relationships – Be An Attractor
- Resilience – Embrace Crookedness
- Renewal – Live to Learn

I realized that the successful people I had been mentored by and had studied were often able to win the toss-ups and flip many of their projected close losses into wins.

Further, it occurred to me that they accomplished this by being better in the three distinct areas of life: they tended to their relationships *by being an attractor*; they overcame difficulties and obstacles with resilience by *embracing the crookedness* of life; and they practiced a habit of constant renewal by *living to learn*.

Fortunately, they had modeled these three approaches for me.

When I thought of the plethora of people I'd worked with who *hadn't* succeeded in reaching their goals, one of these three key areas surfaced as their stopping point. Often they didn't understand the importance of being an attractor, and their relationships simply weren't strong enough.

Others had roadblocks sideline them as they failed to embrace crookedness, or they'd stopped being curious and asking questions – *living to learn* – and were outpaced by the others. Though I had tried many, many things to succeed – and the hundreds of other people I had both observed and read about had, too – I had come to believe that there was the strong possibility that only a small handful of habits could make the difference between winning and losing

So, if it's being an attractor, embracing crookedness and living to learn that are key drivers of success when focused on, how might I translate them to practice?

To summarize:

- To move toward people, **be an attractor.**
- To move through adversity, **embrace crookedness.**
- To grow and keep moving forward, **live to learn.**

Was this approach too simple?

I lean towards simple. Here's why. I learned early on in leading teams that if the path to winning wasn't clear, my people could get lost trying to find it. Or at least waste precious time and energy looking for it. That's why I have always challenged my people to "Drive the Right Five." And here's what I meant.

Corporations tend to get a little nuts about measuring things – this performance measure, that set of results. And while working for P&G with Walmart, I used to study every numbers report that dropped into my inbox.

No prioritizing, no culling out the less useful ones. I wound up so scattered I wasn't able to focus on anything.

Finally, some of the experienced salespeople took me aside. "Not everything we measure matters to the same degree," they cautioned me. "You can get lost in all the reports and numbers. Just look for the key activities that get you the productive results you need."

With this excellent mentoring, I changed my approach to the business and how I led others. I'd work with my team to find the key measures or outcomes that made the difference in our ultimate success, and we focused on those. The rest we deemed interesting, but much less consequential.

My team understood quickly. Whatever helped get to these results was a keeper. Whatever slowed them down or distracted them from these results had to go. We just asked, "What matters to help us win?" and laser-focused on that.

Now, as I looked for a way to settle on success strategies for the Start-up Weekend group, I shifted my exploration from business success to broader success strategies for life, including "Drive the Right Five."

Fewer strategies would be more powerful. Having a short list of powerful habits would make focus and decision-making easier.

I did have to give myself permission to go small and simple. Indeed, it was not just ok; it was preferable. After all, a small rock moving at the right time can trigger an avalanche; a tiny crack can wind up emptying the biggest reservoir.

Sharing the ideas

I gave the kick-off talk to the group of entrepreneurs. One slide; three bullet points. And I was pleased to learn how many grabbed on to the three approaches. Young entrepreneurs with more ideas and energy than cash or experience saw behaviors to adopt that could accelerate their journey to success.

So, I tried the ideas again with other audiences. Though they were mostly informal, I spoke with groups of managers, then C-level leaders. And I found consistently these ideas didn't just work for me or those I've observed. They had usefulness for many levels of experience.

They inspired and created focus. But most of all, because they were so simple, people left believing they could do these three, and better yet, understood how to do them without going back to school for an MBA.

These responses started me on a path of validation, and my version of research. I observed myself more closely and observed others. In time I began to investigate formal behavioral research.

And I found the three approaches I had adopted – be an attractor, embrace crookedness and live to learn – made sense from multiple angles. They made a difference in success at work, but also in parenting, school and life.

How do you go after success?

We all have dreams; achieving them is how we define success. It may be in work, sure. But I think the dreams that matter more come from our lives outside of work – marriage, parenting, friendships, health, and more. Everyone seems to have an opinion about how best to succeed. Who to listen to?

And once that expert is chosen, how do you implement, or keep implementing the system they so aggressively tout? I'd like to suggest you try the three simple approaches explained in the pages ahead.

You'll find you can *become an attractor*, even if you're not a natural charmer.

You can learn to *embrace crookedness*, even if a lot of bad stuff has slowed you down before or uncertainty generates anxiety.

You can find excitement in *living to learn*, even without going back to school.

And small wins with each of these strategies can lead to achieving the goals you've dreamed about.

Part I

BE AN ATTRACTOR

"Your mind is a magnet. You don't attract what you need or what you want; you attract who you are."

—Carlos Santana

1

Don't Just Recruit

As outlined in my book *Get-Real Culture,* one of my most important "ah ha" moments with regard to culture came in 2005. I had just left the telecom giant Sprint to join a spin-off of their wireline division, a new $6 billion company to be known as Embarq.

I'd signed on as president of the Consumer Division, the new company's biggest entity. With around 3,500 employees spread around the country, I knew who I hired for my leadership team was going to be the deal breaker for our ultimate success.

I went to my partner in Human Resources to get searches underway for this stellar team.

"I don't think staffing your direct-report positions is going to be difficult," she told me, "because we've got the strangest thing going on here."

"What do you mean?" I asked, surprised.

"People are lining up to get spots on your Lead Team– and they have made it clear that they don't even care what the jobs are."

"What do you make of that?" I asked her.

"They're telling me they saw how you operated with your Lead Team at Sprint, and they want that experience for themselves," she replied.

Then she laughed a little and proceeded to deliver the powerful message that I will never forget. "It looks like your team-creation strategy consists of being more attractor than recruiter."

Immediately my mind flashed to so many great leaders who had been mentors and models for me, like Walmart founder and CEO Sam Walton. I had seen them almost magnetically draw their team members toward them by their interest and concern.

I knew something different was afoot with these leaders, but until now I hadn't named it. Yep, attracting… that's what they did. I decided to do everything possible to make this part of my operating approach and brand, too.

The advantages

More people wanting to work with me meant the possibility of stronger and better-fitting people on my team. When the talent pool is larger, spotting the types of individuals you're after comes more easily; I knew that from 20+ years of putting together work groups.

Plus, engagement and motivation should come more readily since my Lead Team wouldn't be choosing just a job description or an attractive compensation package. They'd also have pre-chosen me as leader, shortening ramp-up time in growing trust and commitment.

Whatever an attractor was, I could already see the outcomes were going to be helpful. Attracting was something done by a magnet – and described with terms like "pulling in" and "drawing toward." If our energy as a team was already designed to come toward, that meant much more want-to than have-to, more bias toward trust than suspicion, more willingness to engage than to sit back with a skeptical, prove-it-to-me spirit.

With my Lead Team at Embarq, these assumptions proved out. And that Human Resources leader named a quality that's become over time one of the critical three qualities I deem necessary to win.

Besides acting as a staffing magnet, I've seen how being an attractor can provide more options to tip the balance in your favor when results are uncertain and you can be headed for a very close win or loss. Attractors find people want to help them succeed. And attracting can open surprising doors that by rights should be closed.

In the years since 2005, I've been watching for and learning from attractors – understanding better who they are, how they operate, and why this behavior is such a success-accelerator.

A picture of attracting

I have come to describe attractors this way: they're A+ Players and nice.

"What? A+ Players, that I get," you're saying. "But *nice*? Seriously? Has no one ever explained to you that nice guys finish last?"

Calm down. We need to talk about what I mean by nice. Attractors aren't necessarily people with the most Facebook friends or LinkedIn connections. They aren't usually the best-looking, cool, moneyed, athletic types. In fact, research suggests some of these "popular" types are not only not attractors, but often repellers!

In her book, *How to Be a People Magnet*, communications expert Leil Lowndes recounts results of research evaluating popularity among teenagers (and who cares more about being popular than this crowd?). High schoolers were asked to list who they considered popular, then who they liked. The researchers predicted that the people named on the two lists would be the same. After all, doesn't it make sense that popular by definition implies being well liked?

But a surprise lay ahead.

The popular kids were not only absent from the "liked" list; they were actually largely resented by their peers. Eleven percent of the students surveyed said they *despised* the kids voted most popular. It seemed the popular students had *status* because of money or sports prowess or looks or up-front talent. Their popularity came because of this status; not because of likeability.[1]

But the most effective attractors are downright likeable. People seek them because they want to, not because they're afraid of what they'll lose if they don't.

And in a UCLA study, participants rated over 500 adjectives based on how important they were to likeability. Surprisingly the top-rated characteristics had nothing to do with being outgoing, smart or particularly attractive. Instead, the top adjectives related to likeability were sincerity, transparency, and understanding.[2]

That's the kind of "nice" we'll explore together as we talk about what it means to be an attractor.

How can you be both an A+ Player and nice?

Back in the telecom days when cable TV was our most formidable competitor for home phone service, I'm the one who sold 3,500 people on a sales push we dubbed *KCA – Kick Cable's Ass*. (Human Resources insisted we only print KCA on tee shirts and banners…how crass can a Fortune 500 company's language be, after all? But among ourselves, we were clear on which specific part of cable's anatomy we were out to bruise!).

I hope you'll understand from this that winning matters to me. That's why I like A+ players – they're not reluctant to kick some ass on the way to winning. And determination, guts and sheer boldness are often what it takes to win.

But it's *how* they do it that sets attractors apart from plain A+ Players.

Attractors compete against a goal. They push, but they don't push over others to get where they want to go. They make tough calls, but not ones that are tougher on others than on themselves. They're not users or abusers; they look for ways to build others up and bring them success on the way to their own wins and to collective team wins.

Living out this definition of *nice* requires purposeful, courageous choices. It can mean giving the credit that is rightfully yours to another. Or that you decide to hand the mic to someone else on the team, when standing in the spotlight could possibly move you ahead. This take on *nice* means acquiring guts, not losing them.

A young entrepreneur in my city started a small medical device company, and pulled, pushed and prodded it along for five years until a golden opportunity he'd been hoping for presented itself. A very large medical company hired him to provide due diligence for a purchase of a device the company was ready to pay $30 million to acquire.

In the process of investigation, Chris and his team realized there was a far more effective way to accomplish what this device was used for. And without "stealing" any of the technology they'd been paid to evaluate, they went back to their office and brainstormed, designed and built a working model of a new device that was more effective and cheaper than anything on the market…and did this all in eight weeks.

The following week, along with reporting to the large company's leaders about the outcome of their due diligence assignment, they also provided a demo of the product they'd just designed.

"But Chris," one executive said, "I know you understand the value of what you invented here. You could have taken it yourself, produced it, kept us out of the loop and made millions. Why didn't you?"

"That's not the kind of business partners we are," Chris replied. This is an attractor in action. An A+ Player, to be sure. But with a *niceness* that shows itself in courage and generous choices shot through with integrity. There's nothing wimpy or passive or saccharin-sweet in the way attractors "do nice." They leave no wake of destruction on their path to winning; rather, relationships, respect and positive results.

Finding the principles of attracting

Back in the moment when my Human Resources lead named this attractor phenomenon for me, I knew intuitively what she was describing. But when people would ask how to grow as an attractor, I wasn't sure what to tell them.

Was it just a personality some were born with? I was sure that wasn't true, because I knew attractors who were quiet and shy, and others who were so outgoing the party started the moment they walked in the door. Besides, if attracting was just genetic, like brown eyes, how was it I had seen people get better at it as they paid attention and learned?

We could grow into better attractors; I was sure of it. But what was the path? And what were the signposts along that way that would help people know they were on the path?

These questions pushed me to pay attention, not just to the results attractors were generating, but also to how they were doing what they did. How did they behave around people? What choices were consistent? And beyond my own observations, what clues did behavioral science research give to what actions worked better to attract?

I came to three important conclusions. Attractors let others know them; they're not afraid to be vulnerable. They work hard to communicate to others that they matter. And they give others reasons to trust them. From these, I sketched out a path to get you started, or get you accelerating on the way to attracting.

2

Let Others Know You

If you want to be an attractor, forget the advice you've heard about *never let them see you sweat*. Actually, perfect people scare and intimidate us. Openness and vulnerability will take you farther if your goal is truly attracting. Think about sharing more so others can know you.

Let 'em see you sweat

Think about the world of the invincible. No one did Intelligence Agent 007 better than the original James Bond, Sean Connery. "Sweat" was not in his vocabulary.

Ah, but in the 2008 version, played by Daniel Craig, James Bond isn't quite so perfect. Torn between forgiving a former lover who betrayed him and forgetting her because of her treachery, this Bond at times appears unbalanced and emotional. Downright vulnerable.

Did we stomp out of the movie at this disclosure? Hardly. The movie grossed more than $600 million.

Perfection may generate awe, but openness is magnetic and critical to authentic connections with others. Vulnerability draws others to you. It makes you human and relatable...and diminishes fears in others that you'll judge them.

It was a turning point in trust for some of my employees when I publicly admitted a mistake and apologized for it. I had not been watching expenses as closely as I should have been and to get back on track, we were forced into expense reduction mode, which included eliminating unfilled jobs and laying off some people.

Because the responsibility for revenue and expenses stopped with me, the failure was mine. Standard procedure for those of us in leadership during moments like this is often to cover over, reframe, or spin it as something other than what it was. But I couldn't because I expect just the opposite of the people on my team. I want them to trust me enough to tell the truth, even if the truth hurts. How could I do less?

I sucked it up, and in an all-hands meeting, apologized. "Here's what happened," I explained. "Here's why I did what I did, but it caused problems. I'm sorry. And it won't happen again while I'm in charge."

Afterword our connection went to a new level because I was open about a mistake that I had made.

I heard recently about a study evaluating imperfection and likeability in which groups of people were shown two different recordings. In the first, an actor who had successfully answered a bunch of hard questions correctly (obviously smart, right?) then knocked over a full cup of coffee, making a significant mess. In the second version, the same actor came off just as smart, but didn't knock the coffee over. After the videos, each was rated for likeability.

It was the coffee-spiller who was rated significantly more likeable.[3]

Point is, we are all coffee-spillers. Especially me. But to become an attractor, don't try to cover up; let yourself be known in your ups *and* downs, good moments *and* bad, successes *and* mistakes. As a result, others will feel much more connected.

I learned, more than a little to my surprise, that this principle works even in business. I'd expected that "spilling coffee" (i.e. making mistakes) with customers would lead to their taking their business elsewhere.

But at Embarq, we tracked customer tenure and spending data to find out which ones stayed with us and spent more with us. It turns out the most loyal customers – those who stayed with us the longest – were those who had experienced service problems and watched us stepping up to fix them once they made us aware of the issues.

I have learned that others don't expect perfection. If we don't cover mistakes, we attract.

Seek common ground

We connect quicker and more easily to people who are at least a bit like us. For me, connecting came when in an employee meeting, one of my team members asked about my thoughts on work-life balance.

I barely knew what to say. "My family is so much more important to me than work, I don't even think about trying to balance them," I said. "If there's a choice to be made, I choose my wife and children."

"Because of my job," I went on, "you will need decisions, input, and communication from me. And sometimes you'll ask for these responses outside of regular work hours. I've talked with my family about what my availability will be when work hours are done. They come first. They do know, as do my team members, I will respond to work when I can."

Later, I'd be surprised more than once at comments from employees letting me know my clarity in priorities helped free them to follow their own commitment to family with more determination.

And it connected us. Though we shared work, we also shared the daily decisions that come from living full personal lives.

A social researcher asked participants to complete a "profile" of their own personal traits. They were then shown profiles of others that were either highly similar or highly dissimilar to them and asked to select who they'd most like to know. You can likely guess the results. The more similar the trait-match, the more participants said they liked the person profiled.[4]

I work to find similarities by really listening. I remember when I have dropped in on call center reps in their workplace. I'd plunk down in a chair next to a rep and begin asking questions. These inquiries weren't always about their work, but more often about them – their time at the company, their family, their interests. In their answers I was listening for similarities. Did they love any of the same teams I did? Were their kids close in age to mine?

Even though the organizational charts would place us five or six levels away from each other, I knew if we could uncover a similarity or two, the chance of connecting was exponentially greater. And connecting – not evaluating or glad-handing – was my goal.

If you want to attract, let people know you. Don't fear vulnerability. Look for places you and others are alike.

This means, of course, you'll need to be open about yourself – who you are and what your life is like. You'll need to be very willing to be known. When you are, others will let you know them, too.

3

Show Them They Matter

In a 2015 study of components of likeability, participants were matched with a partner, then instructed to complete a brainteaser. Their partner would complete the same brainteaser later in the study, they were told.

After they finished the problem, half the participants received this message from their partner: "I hope it went well. Do you have any advice?" The other half just heard, "I hope it went well."

Those who were asked for advice rated their partners as more competent, and said they'd be more likely to ask them for advice going forward.[5]

Apparently asking for advice doesn't make us look stupid; it makes the advisor think we are smarter!

Think about it. When you ask for my advice, you let me know you see something in me worth pursuing – in what I know, how I think, what I've experienced. You are supporting me by showing I matter to you. For a moment, you've made me guide and teacher. And, I feel valued. How could I not like you more?

This "ask for advice" idea became Survival Mode when I worked at P&G. The company moved me to a new job every 18 to 24 months. This meant learning a completely different brand and category.

Apparently, they figured skillsets transfer and we'd be pushed to learn. They were right on that last one! Often, success depended on our willingness to suck it up, look fairly ignorant, and ask for help.

When you actually need information or advice, don't hesitate to ask! Some of us would rather walk through a bed of hot coals barefoot than admit we don't know everything and ask for another's help. But it's what attractors do when they choose to take the assistance-seeking approach.

And advice-seeking doesn't always have to be about acquiring instructions or problem solutions from others. It can also happen in the way you do casual conversation.

When you are curious about me, and don't stay with the obvious question: "So, what do you do?" Go on to an additional level with, "What seems to be changing in your industry right now?" or "What made you decide that tennis would be your sport?"

When you do this, you are exploring my knowledge and treating me like I know something worth hearing about. People love to talk about their challenges, and I love to hear about these. So I enjoy asking, "What kind of challenges did you have at work this week? What do you find challenging about living in this part of the country? What are the challenges in raising teenagers?"

Ask. Make the call. Send the email. Be the advice-receiver, not always the advice-giver; the question-asker, not always the answer-source. You'll find others around you feel their value, and value you in return.

Stay on the lookout for good

Often we can set our filters so narrowly that we miss greatness in people who are two inches from our noses. And how we see others can influence who they may become.

You may have heard of a widely-referenced study from 1979 in which researchers Robert Rosenthal and Lenore Jacobson created a classroom of elementary students whose IQs had been tested and were very *similar to each other*.

However, the kids' teachers were told a different story. The teachers were given a list of the students in the class who were, the researchers explained, unusually ready to achieve academically.

By the end of the year, IQ testing was repeated on all students. The randomly-selected "ready to bloom" *who in reality had IQs matching their peers*, showed significantly greater gain in their IQ points over their classmates.

Researchers guessed that because teachers thought these students had the most learning potential, they received a greater investment and the results showed.[6]

In other words, *the students became the excellers their teachers thought they were.*

What could this mean for attractors? If you choose to point out the good in others - what you like and things you respond to - chances are greater they'll step up to act in the way you've described them.

This idea came home to me during a time when an organizational leader a level above me came to a senior meeting ready to fire one of his key players.

"Let's put him on the street," the leader said, "and make an example of him to others."

My surprise was probably obvious, because I knew the team member he was describing, and had never seen anything even close to poor performance. So when I left the meeting, I dug deeper and found no one I talked with had performance questions either. I had to wonder if this was simply a personality misfit between a boss and his report, and the consequences seemed unfair to me.

When an opening came up on my team, I asked that the employee in question be transferred to my team. This wasn't the easiest choice for me since I was fairly new to the organization, and the person speaking badly of this employee outranked me. But it seemed to me that fair was fair. The employee came to my team and performed very well. How glad I was that I had chosen to go with the good I believed was there, rather than a negative report.

I know the challenge of choosing to believe the good, especially if you've been burned by believing good about someone who turned out to be a poor performer. I'm not talking about throwing away all good sense and life wisdom.

But there are pieces of good in all of us. If you choose to look for and point out these instead of setting your filter to search for the potentially disappointing, chances are better the people in your life will move toward becoming more of the good you see in them.

But don't just think positively; speak it

I may see positivity in you and even appreciate things you've done or said. But if I don't tell you, how will you ever know you are important?

What you say matters. Negative words do damage, just like your mom used to warn you. But positive words create connections. If you recorded every one of your conversations in a day and evaluated the content, how much of what you said to others would be affirming? Not just neutral ("The weather is good today") but affirming ("That question you asked in the meeting really added clarity.")

And when you don't feel so positive about something someone else has said, maybe something you don't agree with or understand, instead of judging, say, "Interesting. I've never heard it in quite that way. Help me understand. How did you come up with that?"

Instead of a negative judgment shutting down the possibility of relating, you may learn something new, or at the very least come away with understanding of a different point of view you didn't have before.

Open your mouth. Look for things to praise others or be glad about with them – and then tell them. As you make it clear who they are matters, you'll help them see their own value more clearly, and you'll attract.

4

Give Them Reasons to Trust

It's the trust factor that sets attractors apart from simple charmers. Shoot straight. If you can be trusted, others will take chances to follow or help you because they know you aren't nice simply to use them for your own gain. Trust can sound like a lifelong quest, and it is. But I can recommend a simple strategy to grow your trust value.

Stand for the right

Trust grows with truth telling. Few things make me really angry, but you'll see sparks fly if I find I've been lied to. We can like people in our lives who aren't honest, but we know better than to trust them.

It isn't just morality that drives me to value trust so highly; it's also pure efficiency. In the workplace, for example, the higher the productivity, the greater the chance of winning. But productivity goes down when trust decreases; the energy that should be going to creating and executing gets drained off into suspicion, gossip, rumors, and blaming.

During the time I led the retail distribution channel of Sprint, my team met in my office to do a conference call with a major customer on the West Coast. I was working in the office separately, so wasn't directly involved, but I could hear the conversation.

Before long I didn't like what I was hearing. The customer had taken a mean tone and threatened to withdraw his business from us unless the team met demands I knew were different from our contract with his company.

I decided to intervene.

As the customer took a breath in his tirade, I identified myself to him, and said, "So you're basically telling us to take our contract and stick it up our ass. That is not cool."

Complete silence and shocked looks from my team…and complete silence on the other end of the line.

Then, from the customer, "Oh, I think you are misinterpreting…"

I said, "I don't think I misinterpreted it at all. You're saying you are doing this, you are doing that. But this isn't what our contract says."

Silence again, but then the customer backed off. Though he was bullying my team, I had guessed he wasn't really a bully and, once called on his behavior, might adjust. When he did, we found a mutually productive solution.

But this episode made an impression and was a landmark for the team. If they were being treated wrongfully, I'd stand for them, even if it might cost us business. Trust between us grew exponentially that day. Attractors build trust by standing for what is true and right.

A Closing Word of Caution

When you're an attractor, people are drawn to you because they know both your strengths and vulnerabilities, they feel they matter to you, and they believe they can trust you to be straight with them.

But you'd better be real. If you add these behaviors to manipulate others or just to create influence for yourself, not only will you be found out, you'll pay the price.

Organizational behavior researcher Tiziana Casciaro and her team asked 306 adults to remember a time when they had reached out to form a new relationship.

One group was told to recall a time when the person they'd sought out was a professional contact they hoped would help their career.

The other group was asked to think of someone they'd reached out for nothing more than a personal connection with no professional gain expected or intended.

Afterword, both groups performed a word completion task, starting with word fragments like S _ _ P and W _ _ H that could be filled in any way. (For example, STEP or WISH would both be obvious answers).

But the researchers knew from previous studies that feeling morally tainted increases our desires for cleanliness. And sure enough, the group who imagined connecting with others for professional gain created words related to cleanliness, like SOAP and WASH significantly more often than did the group who imagined connecting for nothing more than the joy of relationship.[7]

The act of manipulation created a sense of feeling *dirty*. Attractors aren't manipulators. They genuinely like people and want to be part of their life experience, and to include them in their lives. That's why the power of true attraction can help you build relationships that will make the difference in your success.

Part II

Embrace Crookedness

"Adversity causes some men to break; others to break records."

—*William Arthur Ward*

5

Make Peace

Though I don't spend a lot of time getting wisdom from TV counselors, one nugget from Dr. Phil McGraw of Oprah fame deserves a shout-out.

He said this: "Sometimes you make the right decision; sometimes you make the decision right."

And I was reminded of a maxim taught in one of the country's top MBA programs. They instruct, "Make a great decision, then make it a great decision."

"Harry, has your brain switched over to Yoda-speak?" Legitimate question.

But these quotes stick with me because when I heard them, I knew they'd captured a powerful reason behind my second success approach, that of embracing crookedness.

When we explore how to succeed, we study methods, complete the check-charts, and fill in the blanks with our own circumstances, thinking doing things right will lead to a straight shot at winning. In other words, we imagine life guided by a fastest-way-there GPS that'll map the route with minimal slowdowns.

Here's the problem: life doesn't proceed in a straight line. You'll take four steps forward on that carefully laid-out path and boom! You stumble and break your ankle, or your map falls into the campfire, or an off-the-rails bear decides to plant himself right in your way. Each requires a change in plans and direction to keep going because your success strategy didn't account for this particular schism.

Sometimes these changes are short-lived and fairly easily resolvable, like when your kid gets the flu, delaying a client meeting. But sometimes they hit you like a tsunami in a way that washes away hopes of following the path at all.

A week after you close on the purchase of an expensive house, your boss lets you know a quiet reorganization has been in the works for a number of weeks, and your position will be eliminated. Or you get thrown out of the workspace you planned to lease long-term. Or someone else comes up with and launches a too-similar product just as you were ready to go to market with yours.

Something you didn't expect just crossed your path, demanding you detour or turn back, and you've lost control of a plan you agonized to get right. Reality is, the path to winning (even winning at the margin) is going to be crooked, not straight. And crookedness? It's what actually happens when what you planned for doesn't happen.

You can fight in a heroic attempt to get that carefully-laid plan up and running once again. Or you can sink into a pool of disappointment and despair and slink off, determining not to try something this big again. Or you can curl into a ball of blame: his fault, her fault, their fault, my fault. Precious energy allotted to moving ahead gets siphoned off into distrust, disillusionment and despair.

The question is: if crookedness is a given (as it almost always is!), how will you respond to it? Your answer will make a deal-breaking difference.

Moguls and mountains

Crookedness is personal for me because it's been such a big part of my journey. It's fun to tell a work history as a series of one win after another, but that story isn't mine.

Back in 1999, I was co-owner of a profitable, award-winning small business in Kansas City. For a variety of reasons, I decided to sell my half of the business to my partner and make a move to the booming dot-com world. I moved to and soon became the CEO of a Kansas City-based internet start-up called *uclick*.

Bottom line, that business did not succeed as planned due to the dot-com crash, and I wound up having to lay off over half the company. Then other half was folded back into the mother company. And once that transition was completed, I was out of a job.

You can bank on this: this is not how I planned the *uclick* story would end! Because family commitments required that I stay in Kansas City, I did what I never expected to do. In early 2001 I went back to Sprint where I had been an executive for 5 years earlier in my career, prior to venturing off into the world of small business and dot-com start-ups.

A straight-line path gets crooked. And in the next few years, it got even more crooked.

In 2003, I married Kris and we began to move toward what we expected would be a future filled with joy. But in February 2004, just 6 weeks shy of our first anniversary, medical tests showed Kris had a brain tumor. During surgery the neurosurgeon was able to do a biopsy but not remove the tumor as it is enmeshed in her motor cortex. Unfortunately, the biopsy also showed that the tumor is malignant.

Kris said at the time, "The diagnosis didn't make it true; it made it treatable." But that diagnosis certainly changed everything for us. And it does still as we live life accompanied by the uncertainty that an inoperable, malignant brain tumor creates.

I consider the end of *uclick* in early 2001 as a mogul on the mountainside of life; Kris's diagnosis in 2004 was Kilimanjaro. Both of these situations gave me an opportunity to decide how I'd face the crookedness of life.

In the job change following *uclick*, I was surprised. I found that the "return to Sprint" wasn't so much a repeat as it was an opportunity to take lessons I'd learned about humility and priorities back to a previous company and try again with greater clarity and grace.

And as we faced life in the presence of Kris's diagnosis, we decided to turn "live one day at a time" into much more than just a slogan.

These instances of crookedness changed things dramatically for us, but they definitely didn't take us down! But learning to embrace crookedness isn't natural or easy. We'll look together at some ways to grow in this approach.

Fight or flight

Psychologist Martin Seligman spent more than twenty-five years studying optimists and pessimists. What he learned can be critical for how to respond to crookedness.

Here's the gist. Pessimists tend to believe (a) bad events will last a long time, (b) bad events will undermine everything they do, and (c) bad events are always their own fault. Pessimists imagine the worst ahead – bankruptcy, divorce, dismissal.

Optimists can be confronted with a similarly disappointing circumstance but think about what lies ahead differently. They tend to believe (a) defeat is just a temporary setback, (b) the causes of defeat are confined to this one situation, and (c) defeat is likely not their fault. Circumstances, bad luck, or others could have caused it.

Optimists see unfortunate events in their least threatening light; they see them as temporary and surmountable. So, confronted by a bad situation, optimists see a challenge, and try harder. Seligman references literally hundreds of studies showing that pessimists give up more easily and get depressed more often.[1]

I was lucky early on to experience a powerful lesson in optimism, delivered by my cross-country coach at Vanderbilt. At the beginning of my second season, I developed stress fractures along my right shin. These multiple fractures benched me for the entire season; I had no idea if I'd ever be back to running well or not.

But my coach chose optimism. Instead of shrugging his shoulders and walking away in the face of such a big limiter, he decided I could come back with the right help. He developed a rehabilitation and training schedule for me.

I stuck to the plan and came back the following fall. But I didn't return to the place I'd left off; in a short time I was running better than I had in my last season of performance, and in the spring I ended up setting the Vanderbilt University school record in the 10,000 meters.

My coach saw the crookedness, and said, "How can we use this?" And his rehab plan not only helped in recovery, but it helped me get in better shape – and gave me the confidence to think I really could make a comeback.

There's no way to be optimistic if you're channeling your energy into either despairing over bad events or complaining about the injustice of them happening to you.

And pessimism leads eventually to a sense of helplessness, the belief that nothing you choose to do will improve what happens to you.

Helpless people can't win because their beliefs paralyze them from taking any action at all. If it's not going to make any difference, after all, what's the point of trying?

Making peace with crookedness

Embracing crookedness is about finding peace when circumstances dictate despair. How do you go about learning to embrace the bad stuff in life when everything in you wants to flight or flee?

Three approaches can help as you build your capacity to embrace the things you wish had never happened.

6

Don't Run From Reality

Remember those goofy self-help platitudes once recommended by the gurus where you told yourself, "Every day in every way I'm getting better and better?" Chant them all you want, but behavioral science research says there are much more efficient ways to begin when you've been decked by the crookedness of life.

First, call the disappointment what it is. Don't pretend it didn't happen or jump right over what you are feeling to say it ain't so. Absorb and process, instead of running from reality.

If you wanted the job, and weren't chosen, cuss a little, or wallow a little, or rant a little. If you hurt, say you hurt! Let yourself acknowledge and feel it. Stuffed anger or disappointment doesn't just dissolve; it festers. So, get the process of embracing underway faster by admitting the pain, and feeling it.

But don't get stuck here! Looking the crookedness straight in the face is the beginning, not the end.

Ask productive questions

You can speed recovery time by asking yourself good questions. I've found these three to be useful when I'm dealing with the crookedness of life.

1. *Has anyone ever faced something this bad before?*

This one helps me "normalize" what's just happened and reminds me I'm not the only human on the planet whose been hit like this. Remembering I'm not alone can generate a spark of hope.

2. *Has something like this ever happened to me that wound up working out better than my first plan?*

When crookedness hits, disappointment or uncertainty can cause me to question my own strength and resilience. This question helps me remember this isn't my first rodeo; I've been through tough stuff before and made it. And in some of those situations, the path I was forced to choose worked out better than my original plan. Those recollections can bring renewal.

3. *What if I thought this new challenge might produce something good for me? What would I do next?*

Despair is the ultimate creativity-killer. Using the "what-if" game to introduce the possibility of positive options can get me moving again. And asking myself what I'd do introduces action-planning that can direct the movement productively.

Questions like these can help generate possibilities that were hidden before.

Back in 2012, my partner Jeff and I started a business called *Idle Smart*, manufacturing and selling a product for 18-wheelers that will turn the diesel engine on or off without using the key.

We expected this device would be a major hit with trucking companies whose drivers used sleeper cabs. To stay warm or cool overnight, drivers either had to idle the engine all night – using up diesel fuel – or get up to turn the engine on and off during the night. *Idle Smart's* product would minimize idling and eliminate the driver's need to manually stop and start the engine. The device would monitor the sleeper cab's temperature and automatically turn the engine on and off as needed.

Owners loved that it saved diesel money and was much better for the environment.

But the drivers hated hearing the engine start and stop during the night and didn't want to use it. They had gotten used to having their truck idle all night and, with a driver shortage in the industry, they had a lot of leverage. This set the stage for conflict and dissatisfaction.

But for Jeff and me, this surprise led us to ask one of the questions I've just introduced: *what if this challenge had something good in it?*

Turns out, it did. Truckers had another problem we had not paid as much attention to...until our Plan A was not working well.

If their trucks were not used or turned on over the weekend, the refrigerators and DVD players with which they are equipped would still draw down the battery. There was the chance that Monday morning when the driver wanted to head out for the week, the battery might be dead. And this was a problem!

It's very expensive to jumpstart an 18-wheeler. Plus, this issue increased the chances of missing the first load of the day. This was a problem, as truckers' income depends on hauling as many loads as possible.

As well as starting the truck without the driver present, our device could also measure battery voltage. Our product had the ability to start the engine when it got too low. This charged the battery! Viola! The truck was ready to start on Monday morning and for the scheduled load pickup.

Once we saw the issues with Plan A, which hadn't proved very successful, and began listening for other options, a better direction showed itself.

Here's another example of this principle in action. An astounding 20 billion pounds of produce go to waste on farms every year, largely because supermarkets insist that the products they sell look perfect – uniform sizes, perfectly symmetrical and free of blemishes.

A San Francisco-based company called *Imperfect Produce* was created because someone asked how to make these rejects attractive. They wound up creating a witty and connecting customer experience to people who cared about both the environment and cost and delivered the produce at prices 30% less than their better-shaped cousins.

And here's what I mean by "witty." On the bottom of every produce box, you'll find messages like this: "Wow! If you're reading this side of the box you're either a literate ant, or already repurposing your box for something awesome around the house. Great work! We won't tell you what to make with yours, but we've heard that 1 in 5 cats don't have a fort to play in. Just saying..." [2]

Ecology, economy and playfulness = sales!

If you let yourself get stuck in the disappointment that crookedness can generate, innovative solutions like these won't come to you. And your despair will become a self-fulfilling prophecy.

But with a willingness to acknowledge and embrace crookedness, and then ask questions, today's disappointment might open the way to tomorrow's appointment. You may find there's as much chance this crooked change could work to your advantage as to your disadvantage. That small shift of focus may be just enough to help you take a small step that will tip the balance in your favor.

7

Detour or Dead End?

Crookedness can be a detour to something better, rather than a dead end. It can lead to positive energy rather than annihilation. It can hold promise, rather than poison.

But allowing for this possibility is going to take a decision on your part.

First you must assess the situation fairly. If you decide crookedness can only mean a dead end, you might endure it, or grit your teeth through it, but you won't embrace it and listen for the good it can hold.

Please hear that I'm not underplaying the difficulty of this decision. Failures or hardships, especially if they're enormously costly, can generate emotion that convinces us there's no hope. But history suggests otherwise.

Michael Jordan – named the greatest athlete of the 20th century by ESPN – didn't make his varsity high school basketball team on the first try as a sophomore.

Steven Spielberg was rejected by the University of Southern California film school three times.

The Beatles were rejected by three different record companies before they were signed.

The book *Chicken Soup for the Soul* was rejected by publishers 123 times. The series has now 65 different titles and has sold more than 80 million copies around the world. [3]

Your decision to define a set-back as a detour rather than a dead-end won't come easily, or maybe even right away. But consider it. Once this choice is made, you will find you've set your mind to pay attention to options and opportunities. At that point, you're back on your way to a winning mindset.

8

Reset Your Expectations

Learning how to talk to yourself when you get hit by crookedness is critical. The ability to adjust and reset your expectations can keep you from getting paralyzed by difficulties or failure and moving toward new (and potentially productive) options.

Three productive ways of thinking – and talking to yourself – can pull you out of "fight or flight" and open the way to peace and creativity. Listen to these self-talk examples that can work to your advantage:

1. Tell yourself: "It's not permanent."

Don't let one glitch lead you to expect you'll only see glitches ahead. Failure can be a great seedbed of learning.

2. *Tell yourself: "It's not pervasive."*

Don't globalize – "This experience isn't working as I hoped. That means no experience ahead will ever work as I hope." Or, "I failed in this attempt to lose weight. That means I'll never succeed in taking off these extra twenty pounds and keeping them off so I might as well give it up now." The past isn't the predictor of your future; the best predictor of your future is what you decide to do after disappointment.

3. *Tell yourself: "It's not personal."*

Don't categorically blame yourself. "This isn't working out. I'm so weak. I just don't have what it takes to pull off big challenges." Or "I didn't get the job. They must have decided I just wasn't good enough." In reality, the big challenge, or the job interview might have gone crooked for reasons that had nothing to do with you.

And what if you weren't controlled by negative beliefs about past failures?

Jennice Vilhauer, Ph.D., a psychologist at Emory University studies how people create their futures. When she speaks on expectations, she asks audience members to raise their hands if they want to win the lottery. Nearly every person in the room raises a hand.

Then she instructs, "Keep your hand in the air if in the past month you actually bought a lottery ticket." Not surprisingly, hands drop like flies.

What's the disconnect? People, concludes Dr. Vilhauer, act in light of what they expect to get, not what they want. If you don't expect to win the lottery, you never buy a ticket, and boom! Your expectation proves to be correct. [4]

Her point, of course, is that we wrongly let our expectations of failure (maybe because of past disappointments or painful encounters with crookedness) dictate to us that because we have been disappointed, we will always be disappointed. But what if...

What if we let ourselves believe for a moment there was a chance that we might succeed, even though there'd been failures in the past? What if we allowed that maybe this time we are different because of what we've learned, or the circumstances this time may be different...and a path to winning may open when it didn't before? Changing your mind about what could be can change the game for you.

Reprogram your thinking

Back in my days in sports marketing, our small business did what we knew was very good work helping companies figure out how to use sports advertising and promotions to drive their marketing.

However, we were small, and found that we were about to be dropped by one of our biggest customers because of our size. And our competitors seized on this fact, telling customers, "Yeah, they're good, but they can't handle your complexity and volume of work. Just not big enough."

We'd been focused on the quality of our services; we knew we could deliver. But what about this "size" question? Should we ignore it? Pull back and go after smaller companies? These were the directions our focus on quality would have suggested.

But then we took a shot at reprogramming our thinking. What if we made a stronger platform built on the successes we had had working with large companies? And then, what if we added, "But because we're small, you are going to be special to us, not just another contract." We put together testimonials from the most visible and most satisfied customers we had, along with references and permissions for other companies to call them. Now our message focused on successes, our unique approach, *and* the attention we could provide that larger companies wouldn't. We reprogrammed our thinking and created an approach that worked.

Business consultant Dr. Rick Kirschner in *How to Click with People* uses helpful language to describe what we're talking about when we embrace crookedness.

He encourages people "... to respond adequately and wisely to a situation rather than reacting. Responding rather than reacting isn't nearly as difficult as you might think. Simply notice what is happening and connect yourself to it instead of fighting or withdrawing from it, then find a way to learn from it, leverage it, or leave it behind." [5]

When you're in charge of yourself, you know this is your choice. You realize that your greatest leverage in life is your response to what the moment brings.

A University of Pennsylvania psychology professor gave a personality survey to sales representatives at a major life-insurance agency. He asked – among other things - if, when they met someone, they believed the person would like them. The ones who scored well were called optimists for the sake of the study.

The self-identified optimists had no more training or experience than those life insurance salespeople who were neutral or pessimistic about others liking them. But in the months ahead, the optimists sold one-third more than the less-confident others.

Whoa! The insurance company's senior management took notice – and decided to put this optimistic viewpoint to a tougher test.

They actually hired 100 people as sales reps who had failed the standard industry aptitude exam (yes, you read that right). But these 100 "failures" rated high on optimism. In their first year, these happy failures sold 21% more than the average-optimism sales reps who had passed the aptitude test. And in the second, they sold a massive 57% more. [6]

How do you become one of these bent-toward-winning optimists? Much of the answer has to do with how you respond in the face of crookedness. Don't waste energy rehearsing those Poison Ps:

- *Failing is Permanent*: "Bam! It's just one bad thing after another. Here we go again. I should have known this was coming because stuff I try *always* ends like this."

- *Failing is Pervasive*: "Things went south again. Here's *another thing I don't do well*. When is the list going to end?"

- *Failing is Personal*: "Got it wrong again. This just proves *I don't have what it takes* to make something great happen."

Instead, respond; don't react. When you fail, learn from it, leverage it, or leave it behind.

And, Minimize Whatever Crookedness You Can

We've spent considerable time digging into how to make decisions great, even when they go wrong. But remember the first half of the maxim we began this "crookedness" conversation talking about? It starts like this: "Make great decisions...."

There is something to be said for continually improving decision-making skills! Bad decisions are only bad decisions if you keep making them over and over. But you can stop the cycle by applying principles of decision-making.

Blogger Eric Barker offers science-based answers on how to be awesome at life. And I found his three secrets of making good decisions useful. Here's his direction:

1. *Be sure you're clear on what problem you're trying to solve.*

Generally, you don't need more information to make a good decision; you need the right information. Because of the explosion in technological access to information in the last twenty years, we're drowning in information!

Instead of trying to amass every bit of information you can, focus first on defining the problem *so* you know the right, useful information when you see it.

An executive coach I know claims she gives some of her best help when she interrupts a conversation to ask, *"Exactly what problem are you trying to solve here?"* With that answer clear, next steps to a solution invariably come more quickly.

2. *Ask yourself, "What advice would I give to someone else in this situation?"*

Creating an outside perspective on your situation will help you think with more distance, and lessened investment so often the answer comes quicker and with more clarity.

3. *Make a 'good enough' decision.*

Trying to make the perfect choice overwhelms your brain and makes you feel out of control. And you want science for this? Eric Barker quotes a neuroscientist who explains, "Trying for the best, instead of good enough, brings too much emotional ventromedial prefrontal activity into the decision-making process. In contrast, recognizing that good enough is good enough activates more dorsolateral prefrontal areas, which helps you feel more in control." [7]

Brain techno-specifics aside, if you hold out for perfect, in reality there is no such thing in decision-making.

Remember where we started in this "crookedness" exploration? *Make a great decision, then make it a great decision.* And the only reason the second part of the challenge is necessary is because even great decisions aren't perfect. You'll take away stress by not pushing yourself for perfection and letting good enough simply be good enough.

And when the decision is behind you, just embrace whatever crookedness lies ahead.

You can't escape crookedness, no matter how good you are at careful planning, or self-discipline, or keeping all your ducks in a row. Most of life's crooked places are simple jabs that just hurt a little, but others are such major body blows they can bring you to your knees.

Either way, a commitment to embrace rather than fight them will help you focus energy on either fixing them or using them to bring more good to your life than could have existed had they never happened and will help keep you moving toward winning.

Part III

LIVE TO LEARN

"Live as if you were to die tomorrow. Learn as if you were to live forever."

—Mahatma Ghandi

9

The Power of Learning

Here's when the power of learning came into focus for me during my stint in Northwest Arkansas working for P&G with Walmart.

In the world of business, we're all about setting measurable goals, sales projections, and production targets. How many calls do we expect the reps to make per hour? What profitability increase do we expect this cost-saving measure to produce?

When these numbers come in, they provide fodder for good questions, especially if results aren't as we expected. I saw this in action when the Walmart team reviewed a graph showing sales over a 53-week period. It looked as we expected – except for a sales slump during a specific week. That result was confusing and seeing it reflected in the data before us generated questions. Why was this week so soft for sales? Did a competitor do something that drove this?

Poking a bit led to useful learning. That week the East Coast had been hit with a hurricane, which greatly impacted sales activity in the region. Everyone's business was impacted, not just ours.

Evaluating that chart didn't give us a ready answer. But it generated questions that allowed us to learn something we needed to know about how the business ebbed and flowed. Probing to know what we didn't know gave us new understanding about the impact of a weather anomaly on sales and equipped us to better pay attention and predict impact when the next odd weather pattern developed.

Having some expectations of what ought to happen helped us ask, "What happened here? What's going on? What might we be missing? What's to learn from this?"

Reviews like this are probably common in your workplace. But do you use this same technique to discover what you don't know in other areas of life?

I even take what I call "the smell test," as in, "something doesn't smell right here…" to more mundane levels.

When driving to a Royals game, for example, I hit a spot where traffic was backed up so significantly I had to wind through side neighborhoods to make it to the game on time. But instead of complaining about the traffic snafu, my curiosity kicked in.

What could have caused this back up, since it had never happened before on our game drives? An accident? Road construction I hadn't been aware of? Some other anomaly – like a marathon route that goofed up traffic?

Again, would getting an answer to this traffic quandary change life as I know it? Nope. But I choose to use these situations as incentives for curiosity rather than complaining. By doing this, I find myself more present in real life. And more often than not, I wind up learning something. And occasionally, what I learn can prove to be more useful than I would have ever guessed.

I often improve outcomes by paying attention to how I expected things around me were going to function – and then asking questions when I see a deviation. It's an easily acquired, practical habit that can open surprising doors.

As you head for success, you'll find that learning is one of your best tools.

10

Listen to Fresh Voices

When I came to the Walmart customer team, representing P&G, we spent considerable time working on demand-and-supply issues, since having the products on the shelves when customers need them is critical to customer satisfaction and sales. Because one line of products I represented was our cold and flu treatment line, stuff like Nyquil, Vicks VapoRub and Chloraseptic, it occurred to me that a new approach might be possible. I knew, though my Walmart partners didn't, that P&G tracked cold outbreaks across the country, using Centers for Disease Control data.

It occurred to me that if Walmart could have information on the areas where colds and flu were just starting to increase, we could ship larger pallets of medicines to these areas, allowing stores to be better prepared for an influx of customers looking for these products.

After some deliberation, the Walmart buyer agreed to this proposal; it turned out to be very successful for both companies. And it happened because Walmart was willing to retune, listen to fresh voices and even include someone from the outside.

When you set out to learn, do you always go to the sources you, well…always go to? Does your research always follow a predictable pattern? I've learned the hard way that listening to conventional wisdom can sometimes lead to failure.

When we were deciding how to sell our *Idle Smart* product, we asked others for advice. Since the product was designed to limit the idle time of 18-wheelers, we were strongly encouraged to sell the product through local and regional dealers. Going around the well-established, powerful dealer network could even undermine our success, we were told. This was because these folks can be quite competitive and expect to be the first place anyone selling new "truck stuff" comes.

This tried-and-true perspective was a mistake for us. In the dealer network we were competing for attention with hundreds of other products. And it wasn't easy for dealers to represent us well because a new product like ours took some training to understand and explain its benefits.

Our sales success didn't take off until we decided to skip the dealer route and go directly to the trucking companies. Doing what others saw as the reasonable route didn't work. But when we choose instead to listen to different opinions, new options emerged.

Fresh voices can come in book form

Not all fresh learning has to come from face-to-face conversations. I learn continually from the captured conversations we call "books." Because I was a history major, business history pulls me in. And as I read, I'm not looking for a record of successes and failures; I read to uncover the critical issues that led to success or failure.

And I'm not alone in this learning methodology.

Tesla CEO Elon Musk reportedly read through the *Encyclopedia Britannica* when he was nine years old, and he was known for reading some ten hours a day. His tastes tended to science fiction novels, but you could argue he turned this penchant for imagination into unusually strong business success.

Microsoft founder Bill Gates reads a book a week. Most are nonfiction – public health, engineering, business, science – but an occasional novel gets thrown in, too.

Berkshire Hathaway magnate Warren Buffet spends five to six hours a day reading five different newspapers.

Oprah Winfrey credits reading as her "personal path to freedom." She said, "Books allowed me to see a world beyond the front porch of my grandmother's shotgun house." She credits books with giving her the power to see possibilities beyond the limits placed on her at the time.

Dallas Mavericks owner Mark Cuban often reads three hours a day to learn more about the industries he works in – a habit he developed early in his career. "Everything I read was public," he said. "Anyone could buy the same books and magazines. The same information was available to anyone who wanted it. Turns out most people didn't."

But Cuban did, and did the work to go after it, so success followed.[1]

Turn the problem on its head

Swiss psychiatrist and adventurer Bertrand Piccard had an obsession with circling the globe by balloon. (Some have wondered if his determination about this crazy goal suggested he needed to see a psychiatrist himself, but that's a story for another day.) In a third attempt, he completed the feat in twenty days. So far, so good.

At journey's end, as he waited seven hours in the Egyptian desert to be picked up, he thought about how much of his time during the experience he had spent worrying about running out of the liquid gas that kept his balloon aloft. Obviously, he'd become adept at managing fuel; otherwise the feat would never have been completed. But as he wondered if there might not be better ways to manage fuel than he had discovered so far, a new thought came to him.

What if there could be a way to fly round the world without any fuel on board at all? The next time he set out to circle the globe, his craft was a *fully solar-powered* plane. [2]

I saw this happen when the P&G/Walmart customer team's conversation centered on improving their distribution center processes. I perked up at questions about distribution centers, because P&G provided Walmart with a whole lot of paper products (think Bounty paper towels, Charmin toilet tissue and Pampers) – and clearly these are all bulky, demanding significant space in a distribution warehouse.

In the aftermath of this conversation, I watched genius happen. The discussion had centered on Walmart's scanner data. By combining their individual store scanner and cash register information, we were told, a store employee can see quickly how much of a specific product to order.

Another P&G employee broke in. "Is there any way we could get that information directly to our manufacturing plant versus sending it through the distribution center?"

The room got quiet in the way bumping into a whole new idea leaves you quiet. The answer was...yes!

As a result of developing and experimenting with the idea, Walmart started shipping these paper product orders directly from the P&G manufacturing facility, cutting out the Walmart distribution centers altogether. Point-of-Sale data went directly from Walmart to P&G and product shipments headed out to the stores much more quickly and efficiently.

Finding a new combination for two ideas – store sales data and manufacturer's shipping plans – led to a new efficiency. One way you can turn a problem on its head is by noodling for unexpected combinations and ask what new ideas they might offer.

Zen and the Art of Motorcycle Maintenance, a multi-million seller back in the 1970s, took this tack. By cleverly combining two unrelated ideas like zen and motorcycles, author Robert Pirsig helped people sit through philosophical discussions about approaches to life that most of us would never endure if they'd come to us the way they did in those college philosophy classes.

Publishers use this idea all the time. Check these book titles. How about *Bouncing Forward* or *The Upside of Irrationality*. Doesn't everyone know the expression is "*bouncing back*?" And how could irrationality have an upside? But turning a phrase like this on its head pushes the upside-down thinking that feeds curiosity.

Think of the first pro football player to sign up for a ballet class. Or the first designer to combine sleek, stainless kitchen appliances and fixtures with barn board cabinets and old brick floors?

These now seem like obvious combinations to us. But someone with a challenge had to first look at *this*, then over at what looked like an unrelated *that*, and put them together to create something different and better

Change the time frame

You can also turn a problem on its head by thinking long term rather than the more obvious short-term. This came clear at Embarq when we decided to create a "price for life" offer for our residential high-speed data product. If you signed on for a certain internet speed, we guaranteed that price for that speed would never increase.

This was fairly revolutionary, since internet providers typically make money by luring in new customers with low, low introductory prices, then after the customers have settled in using the service, raising the price. And to some of our folks in finance, it seemed like the offer was unwise.

In the long run, here's how it proved profitable. The high-speed internet our customers were buying – and getting a guaranteed "price for life" – was very, very good at the time. But as you know, internet speeds increase all the time. So in the next few years, large numbers of these customers with the "price-for-life" guarantee upgraded to faster speeds.

We kept our promise; if they stayed with the speed they'd chosen initially, the price never increased. But most didn't, so the plan proved very successful and profitable as our churn (customers leaving) dropped dramatically. It was simply a question of looking long-term rather than at just today's or tomorrow's return.

How about you? If you are pushing yourself to grow as a learner, you'll find new opportunities if you play with unexpected combinations of resources, ideas or time frames. You never know what new insight will surface.

11

Ask the Right Questions

Remember the Polaroid camera? The inspiration for it was a three-year-old child's question. When inventor Edwin Land's daughter didn't want to wait to see the vacation photos her father was taking, a kid's "why not?" question prompted a new invention.[3]

You'll learn faster if you free up your imagination from the limits of how things have always been and start asking "why," "why not" and "what if." Deciding to abandon what is known as "functional fixedness" – limiting objects or solutions to the uses you've always seen in action – creates room for new thinking. You can often refine and make progress by asking the right questions.

For example, remember when we assumed the only kinds of public transportation that could move people around an urban area were taxis, buses, subways, and trains? Then someone said, "Why not bicycles you can rent?" And then, "If bicycles, why not electric scooters?"

Here's another example.

Back in 1976, an Arizona State University broadcasting student named Van Phillips was injured in a water-skiing accident when a motorboat ran into him and cut off his left foot and leg just above the ankle. An artificial limb allowed him to get around on his own without crutches, but the athletic, active life he'd enjoyed as a pole-vaulter and springboard diver looked like it was over.

But Phillips was determined to find a way to run – and even jump – again. He left behind his broadcasting studies at ASU for Northwestern University's Biomedical Engineering program and began work on designing an artificial limb that had the strength, resilience and flexibility to allow the wearer to run and jump.

He started by asking "what if…". *What if* an artificial limb didn't have to look like a human leg?

Inspired by the C-shape of a cheetah's hind leg, Phillips developed an initial design that eventually became the device you now see on 90% of Paralympian athletes and many others. The L-shaped foot he designed created a "heel" that acted like a spring so the wearer could push off with each step. Now running and jumping were possible. [4]

Today we don't see this design as strange. But in its first conceptions, the thought that amputees would have a "leg" that didn't look at all like a leg was not on the table.

Invite others' questions

Those who more easily ask "what if..." often are freer to do it if they are solving a problem outside their area of expertise. For example, the drive-through concept used by McDonalds and most every other chain in the US was based on the principles of a fast Formula 1 racing pit stop. The first foldable lightweight baby stroller was inspired by a retired aeronautical engineer, using the concept of an airplane's retractable landing gear. [5]

"What if..." and "why not..." aren't as hard to ask if you have less invested, or fewer habits engrained into present, obvious solutions. When you're out to learn, ask for input from someone who doesn't deal regularly with the problem you're trying to solve. Counterintuitive? Yes, because we believe so deeply that experience is everything. But experience can also be an inhibitor if your goal is to learn, and to create something new. If you're not learning from your usual sources, look for sources you wouldn't usually tap – and see what responses the "what if..." and "why not..." questions call up from them.

Keep an open mind

Resist quick judgments. When you say this or that is boring, you're closing off a possible place of new learning. Instead, you might ask, "Why isn't that interesting to me? Who does find it interesting? What would they say they love about it?"

Looking at the world with openness lets new learning flourish. For example, a friend of mine has zero interest in football. But when she picked up a business-coaching client who was a former player for the New York Jets, she was pushed to learn.

A woman who couldn't tell you what a wide receiver did found that, in a game she considered boring, there were great analogies for business and growth that connected to some of her clients in ways her other illustrations hadn't. And she became a better business coach.

But her prejudices about what could and couldn't interest her might have kept her from useful learning if she hadn't been pushed into new territory.

Part of our reluctance about this "open mind" idea has merit. You don't have to live long to find that if something can go wrong, at some point, it will. Or at least this is what it often feels like.

But what if, instead of allowing fear to dominate, when you hit uncertainty you chose to define it as an opportunity for curiosity? "Hmmm. Some place I haven't been before. A problem I've not solved before. A conflict I've never faced before. There's going to be some great learning here!"

Of course, I'm aware unbridled optimism can be just plain stupid. See a car barreling toward you, and step in front of it...stupid. Get an email promising that for a hefty fee you'll get the chance to collect funds on deposit in your name in a bank in Ghana...stupid.

But because these "far end of the continuum" dangers exist, don't we too often judge every new circumstance as too risky? I know I'm tempted. But I find that asking, "Could this be a valuable chance to learn?" consistently moves me more quickly to the posture of curiosity that I want to maintain.

And an idea to add...to stimulate curiosity, just do something different. Drive a new route to work. Try almond milk. Have lunch at an Ethiopian restaurant. Listen to country music, or Mozart if you're already stuck on Kenny Chesney. Try calling instead of texting for a day to see what you observe. Take the bus.

Ignorance often isn't lack of information; it's selective awareness – choosing only to notice a certain set of facts, or the opinions of a certain group of people, or relying too much on default thinking to make your decisions.

And it can be fueled by what psychologists call "confirmation bias" – looking for information that supports your beliefs rather than evidence suggesting you are wrong.

Want to avoid ignorance? Keep an open mind!

And keep asking questions

I've often spoken with great admiration about the manager of our customer call center who let her people text and play games on their phones while talking to customers, so long as customer needs were met. With this strategy she kept customer satisfaction high while increasing employee satisfaction and, thus, dramatically reducing employee turnover. But let me tell you a part of the story that deserves a place in a conversation about consistent learning.

That manager found that solution – one which worked outrageously well for us, by the way, in terms of employee productivity and retention – because she asked a question and kept asking when the answer didn't come quickly.

The question came when she saw her kids juggling several tasks at once – doing homework, texting, watching

TV, and staying in a conversation. She asked herself, "How are they managing all this?"

A clear answer never came, but this mystery led her to a different question: "If my kids can do this, could my call center reps do it, too? Might they be able to work effectively with customers and also be multi-tasking – texting, messaging or playing Solitaire?"

I'll admit, my initial answer was, "Absolutely not!" But the manager experimented with surprisingly (to me!) good results, then launched the new, more flexible, employee guidelines. Point is, she asked a question, and kept asking until it led to fresh creativity.

Captain Chelsey "Sully" Sullenberger became a hero when he safely landed a commercial aircraft carrying 155 passengers in the Hudson River. But this "once in a lifetime" moment was one he'd actually been preparing for most of his career by building a habit of learning. He was a flight leader and training officer in the Air Force. Sully was so invested in safety, he eventually became an accident investigator.

Although commercial flights are almost always routine, every time his plane pushed back from the gate, he would remind himself that he needed to be prepared for the unexpected.

"What can I learn?" he would think.

When the unexpected came to pass on a cold January day near New York City in 2009, Sully had a mental data bank ready with options for what he could instantaneously consider because of the learning exercises he'd imposed on himself during all those takeoffs.

He successfully fought the tendency to grab for the most obvious option (landing at the nearest airport) and chose the one more likely to bring success. [6]

Captain Sullenberger taught himself to live in a habit of learning, and it paid off for hundreds and their families.

12

Mine Your Mistakes

A mistake is only a true failure if you don't learn from it. Train yourself to mine your mistakes for key learnings – the nuggets of gold – and repurpose them into your revised plan.

As a student at Vanderbilt, I ran cross-country and track. Because I'd finished the 10,000-meter race in 31 minutes and 11 seconds, I thought I had it in me to break 31 minutes. And I also knew how to get there. I needed to moderate my pace during the first half of the race to still have enough stamina during the second half to finish strong.

The race day came when I had targeted to break my personal best. The starting gun went off, and so did I. Unfortunately, too fast. Sure enough, by the second half of the race, I didn't have enough energy to keep up my targeted pace. I failed to reach my sub 31-minute goal.

The lesson for me turned out to be deeper and more long-lasting than just a reminder to stick with my plan and take the first half of the race at a reasonable pace. I realized I'd messed up on pacing because I let all that super-charged excitement of competition replace simply focusing on the goal. My emotional diffusion muddied the clarity about what mattered most, and I lost out.

I've applied the learnings from this lesson over and over. And it's helped me win when the stakes were much higher than a long distance running personal record.

Mistakes can become friends if you pay attention and listen to what they're trying to tell you. Failure became the stimulus to move toward eventual success.

Five Advantages of Curiosity

Curiosity has power. It can open new worlds and enhance the passion and productivity you experience in life. As you grow as a learner, you'll be equipping yourself with this power when the time comes to tip that scale toward success.

May I leave you with my five highest-motivating advantages to being relentlessly curious?

1. *Curiosity awakes your powers of observation.*

   Did you notice that the last time you bought a different car – maybe an SUV instead of that sedan you always chose – that all you see on the road are SUVs? Does this mean the entire car market suddenly shifted? No. It's that your decision to commit to an SUV has awakened your awareness of these vehicles; now you see them everywhere!

   This capacity to awaken perception comes to play when you choose curiosity. Once you ask yourself, "I wonder what it takes to become a host through AirBnB," you'll find yourself noticing the world around you differently. People who mention they've rented their houses will stand out or sharpen in your senses. You'll overhear conversations you've ignored before or think of people who have not come to mind in a while who once did this.

2. *It will make you smarter.*

   In one study highly curious children aged three to eleven improved their intelligence test scores by twelve points more than their least-curious counterparts did.[7]

3. *Curiosity increases perseverance.*

   Merely describing a day when you felt curious has been
   shown to boost mental and physical energy by 20% more
   than recounting a time of profound happiness.

4. *It keeps your mind active instead of passive.*

   Like a muscle that's finally getting used, that "muscle"
   inside your skull gets stronger. Those neuropathways in
   your brain strength as curiosity drives you to ask
   questions and poke for answers.

5. *It leads to better decisions in the future because you will
   have acquired more data from which to draw
   conclusions.*

   Learning continually – living to learn – will keep you
   growing continually and make you unstoppable as you
   move toward success.

Epilogue

Grinding Your Way to Success

Every year for the past 25 years a bunch of friends mostly from our days at P&G have gathered in Myrtle Beach for a four-day golf trip. And as guys do, everyone has earned or been given a nickname.

Mine? *"Grinder."*

These friends who know me so well hit it right on the money. "Grinder" fits me because that's what I do.

I believe I have succeeded because I grind…and grind…and grind. I just keep at it and refuse to quit. I'm not talented enough to win early and often by most scorekeeping, but I relentlessly, optimistically just keep plowing forward. I do small things longer or better than others; I keep grinding because this often enables me to win at the margin.

Grinding academically

Here's what I mean. I completed my undergraduate and graduate degrees without a break, so I spent six consecutive years going to classes. In those six years, I never once skipped a class. Of course, I occasionally attended tired or hung-over, but I still went.

This choice had nothing to do with wanting some non-existent "perfect attendance" award. Rather, early on it occurred to me that the likelihood was extremely high that when professors decided what to talk about in class, they'd pick material they'd most likely choose when it came time to design the test.

Brilliant, right? Not really. Just pragmatic.

I figured that if I went to every class, listened, and took notes that I could review just before the test, I'd increase my chances of success. It worked.

I graduated with honors from Vanderbilt University and in the top handful in my class from the Kelley MBA program at Indiana University.

I didn't achieve these goals because I studied the hardest or was the smartest. It was because I just kept showing up and paying attention hour-by-hour, week-by-week, year-by-year.

Grinding athletically

The same unglamorous strategy worked in athletics. I learned early on I'm not talented enough for team sports, and

I don't do well with the focus required for ball-and-stick sports like baseball or golf.

However, I found a place for myself in long-distance running. This sport requires little expertise or finesse – you largely just have to keep at it. Again, during the running season at Vanderbilt, I didn't skip practice or weasel out of commitments I made to lift weights. And during my college running career, I set the Vanderbilt University school record for the 10,000 meters that stood for thirty-five years.

Grinding in business

When I went back to work for Sprint as a VP in the Consumer Long Distance Division following my unsuccessful stint in the dot-com start-up world, our president was a leader named Tim Kelly. After I had been on the team for a year, Tim got moved to another role in the company. While looking for his replacement, the Sprint leadership designated me interim president. There was clarity in the appointment that "interim" wasn't a code word; it was made clear I didn't have the experience to lead such a large division, so I'd be filling in until someone more experienced could be found.

I asked myself, "What should I do with this opportunity?" I could simply maintain what "is" and try to not embarrass myself while I was in the spotlight, in hopes that later – if I didn't make any grand mistakes – I might be promoted to a larger challenge.

Or maybe I should take the opposite tack in this one-in-a-lifetime opportunity, and go after a grand gesture, a big splash, a career-defining initiative. I'd definitely have a bigger chance of getting noticed, and maybe snagging this significant position for the long-term.

However, those years of "grinding" made the decision for me. I wouldn't do nothing, but I also wouldn't risk everything to shine.

Just as I'd done academically and in sports, I'd look carefully at the landscape and identify the places where I could influence success.

I studied the factors that most powerfully drove our business results and paid careful attention to making adjustments and accountabilities that tweaked these to produce even better. I asked questions about the culture – how easy it was to get work done, and how much people felt invested in working there – and again, drew from twenty years of business experience to make changes in the places I thought could make the biggest difference in joy and production.

These changes I instituted weren't the flashiest; they didn't need to be, because my predecessor had been a very strong leader. But like the grinder I am, I made sure they didn't stop with strategy slogans and "value posters," but were actually implemented with accountability. In other words, without a lot of fanfare, I put my stamp on the organization.

Six months into instituting these changes, Sprint asked me to become president of the division. And in another eighteen months, I was moved to president of another major division. Not long after, I was asked to be President of the Consumer Markets division at Embarq when it was spun off from Sprint. Those six months of "grinding" proved to be the game changer in my career.

Success may be just another try away

Inventor and genius Thomas Edison once said, "Many of life's failures are people who did not realize how close they were to success when they gave up." Edison was the brains behind five different multibillion-dollar fields: electricity, motion pictures, tele-communications, batteries, and sound recording. His work resulted in 1,093 US patents. And though we can't say enough about his genius, we might do well to praise Thomas Edison as the "Guru of Grinding."

For example, with his work on the light bulb, Edison came late to the game. Twenty-three others had already invented early versions which were in use commercially to light streets and buildings. The field was crowded. Yet Edison won.

How? His team spent a year doing thousands of experiments until they succeeded in the creation of a light bulb for everyday home use. They simply kept at it, over and over again, until a solution surfaced.[1]

Genius? Or grinding? It may be a combination, but simple cleverness without the sweat of persistence wouldn't have created this game-changing accomplishment.

Ignore the gorilla

Grinding means you don't get pulled away by every distraction that comes along; you stick to what's at hand. And this kind of focus has great power.

Two Harvard psychologists studying attention created a now-famous video that tells much about the power of focus. In this video, six men and women, half in black tee shirts and half in white ones, were given a basketball and told to pass it back and forth among themselves.

Participants were asked to count how many times the players wearing the white shirts passed the basketball. At the end of the short video, an announcer asked how many passes were counted, and the subjects reported, expecting praise for their observational success.

But then the announcer asked, "Did you see the gorilla?" Turns out halfway through the game, a person in a gorilla costume came to the middle of the screen, beat his chest and walked off.

In experiments repeated with people of all ages and background, starting with the Harvard students, at least half missed the gorilla. They got so busy counting passes they simply overlooked the other, much more dramatic, action right in front of them.[2]

Pay attention to your **Why**

What you choose to pay attention to matters. It can actually block out fairly powerful distractions and keep you grinding to success. Question is, what should that attention-grabbing focus be?

I'd suggest you will increase your chances of margin-winning successes if you focus on your *why*.

Back in 1983, Steve Jobs was trying to entice John Sculley to leave a wildly successful career at PepsiCo to become Apple's new CEO. Jobs reportedly asked him, "Do you want to spend the rest of your life selling sugared water or do you want a chance to change the world?"

Sculley took the job with meaning and became part of a company focused on changing the world. [3]

How about you? Can you say *why* you're doing the work you're doing? Does the *why* have personal meaning to you? And do you review it more than just once a year when you're setting those New Year's resolutions?

If you are clear on your *why* and keep it in front of you, you can stay with washing pots and pans, or messing with out-of-sync coding, or a million other mundane grinds. They can keep your attention, if you've chosen to focus on your motivation.

Are you a dishwasher to keep your kids in the school that gives them their best shot at success? Does the code you write help a health-insurance enterprise make life easier for people in illness? Remind yourself of these motivators and grinding gets easier.

Knowing your **Why** *brings power*

With so much empty talk about values, a challenge to clarify and claim your own motivation can feel fake and far-removed. But this kind of clarity keeps me working with more energy than I would find without it.

For example, work as CEO of a refractive eye surgery company meant in the macro that I was part of helping people get their best view of the world and those they loved. But it also gave me work I enjoyed ten minutes from my house, so I could be available to my family and part of their lives in the way I want to.

Reminding myself of these two drivers made work mean something more than a paycheck and helped give motivation to make the daily work as good as it could be for everyone in the company, and for our customers too.

If you can hold your personal *why* clearly in view, you'll keep the focus on what matters. And all those noisy, smelly gorillas that wander onto the scene, beating their chests and snorting, will be out of your view.

Keep on grinding when the odds look impossible

In 2016, the English soccer club Leicester City was given a 5,000-to-1 chance of winning the Premier League championship. These are about the same odds bookmakers would give to Bono becoming the next pope.

To understand how completely impossible this win was, it helps to know that in the Premier League, the same four teams had won the championship for the previous 20 years. The closest little Leicester City had ever come to winning was finishing second...back in 1929! And in the 2015 season they had lost so many games they barely escaped being tossed out of the league completely.

This is generally not the stuff of champions.

Yet at the end of the 2016 season, Leicester City took the top trophy.[4] Pundits came up with all kinds of explanations, but the reason was never completely clear.

But one thing is clear. If the Leicester City team had stopped grinding it out, there would have been absolutely no hope for a win.

If you want to see the scales of success tip in your favor, you don't ever quit. Keep grinding. You can change your odds of success.

A Get-Real Mindset and You

Remember the premise we started with? It anchored success in three very simple easy to understand areas – relationships, resilience and renewal –and the associated approaches for each.

Relationships grow as you **become an attractor**.

Resilience strengthens as you **embrace crookedness**.

Renewal happens continually as you **live to learn**.

Consistent, small wins in these arenas can help you grow the mindset that leads to success.

Persevere – keep grinding. As you do, you dramatically increase the odds of winning the toss-ups and flipping the losses. Most importantly, I believe you'll set yourself on a path to a life with the odds of success in your favor.

May you go on to achieve that success in all the ways that matter most to you.

Acknowledgements

This is the third book I have published, and once again a bulk of the credit for getting to the finish line goes to my awesome ghost writer, Maureen Rank. Maureen takes my thoughts, stories and ramblings...and (amazingly) organizes them in a way that is coherent, memorable and "on brand" for me. I owe her so much for helping make my speaking business successful over the past eight years...starting with the publishing of *Get-Real Leadership* in 2012, continuing with *Get-Real Culture* in 2016 and concluding (probably!) with *Get-Real Mindset* in 2020.

February 6, 2020, marked the 16th anniversary of Kris' brain tumor diagnosis. By the grace of God and against the odds, she is going strong. I don't question why or how; I simply celebrate.

A big part of the celebrating comes in the form of fundraising for the *Head for the Cure Foundation* via *Get-Real* keynote speaking and book sales. At the end of 2019, *Get-Real* exceeded $400,000 net raised and donated to *Head for the Cure* from speaking fees and book proceeds, and I do not intend to slow down.

This book is a bit different than my first two. It is, purposefully, more focused on *life broadly* than on *business specifically*. Because of this shift in focus, I had much more fun with the research, storytelling and writing process. And, as a result, I believe it is applicable to a far greater number of people. Enjoy.

About the Author

Harry S. Campbell is a highly respected speaker on the subject of leadership and culture. *Get-Real* is the philosophy that has guided his successful 35-year business career.

Known for his high energy, genuine approach and storytelling, Harry commands attention and leaves his audiences inspired to take "real" action.

Harry has been a president for two Fortune 500 companies, co-owner of an award-winning small business, CEO and board member of an Internet start-up, and founding member of the industry-changing Walmart-P&G Customer Team in Northwest Arkansas.

He has driven exceptional people and business results in a broad range of industries from consumer packaged goods and telecommunications to sports marketing, digital media and refractive eye surgery.

Harry lives with his wife, Kris, and their youngest child in Overland Park, Kansas. He is an avid Indiana Hoosiers fan, an active member in the United Methodist Church of the Resurrection and a fervent supporter of the *Head for the Cure Foundation*. Harry is passionate about motivating and inspiring people to make a positive impact in their lives, businesses and communities.

You can learn more at www.harryscampbell.com.

References

Part II

1 – Leil Lowndes, *How to Be a People Magnet*, (McGraw-Hill Education, 2002).
2 – Travis Bradberry, "Thirteen Habits of Exceptionally Likeable People," *Forbes*, (January 27, 2015).
3 – Richard Shotton, "Why Admitting a Weakness Makes People Like You More," *Association for Psychological Science*, (February 21, 2018).
4 – Patrick King, *The Science of Likeability*, (Createspace, 2017).
5 – Alison Wood Brooks and Francesca Gino, "Asking Advice Makes a Good Impression," *Scientific American*, (March 1, 2015).
6 – Robert Rosenthal and Lenore Jacobson, *Pygmalion in the Classroom*, (Crown House Publishing, 1992).
7 – David Burkus, *Friend of a Friend*, (Houghton Mifflin Harcourt, 2018).

Part III

1 – Martin Seligman, *Learned Optimism*, (Vintage Press, 2006).
2 – Dan Gingiss, "How Imperfect Produce Turned Ugly Fruit and Vegetables into Marketing Perfection," *Forbes*, (April 28, 2019).
3 – Jennice Vilhauer, "Why the Fear of Disappointment is Detrimental to Your Life," *Psychology Today*, (September 27, 2017).
4 – Jennice Vilhauer, *Think Forward to Thrive*, (New World Library, 2014).
5 – Rick Kirschner, *How to Click with People*, (Hyperion, 2011).
6 – Keenan, "The Proven Predictor of Sales Success Few Are Using," *Forbes*, (December 5, 2015).
7 – Eric Barker, "This is How to Make Good Decisions: Four Secrets Backed by Research," *Observer*, (July 2, 2016).

Part IV

1 – Chris Weller, "Nine of the Most Successful People Share Their Reading Habits," *Business Insider*, (July 20, 2017).
2 – Cyril Bouquet, Jean-Louis Barsoux and Michael Wade, "Bring Your Breakthrough Ideas to Life," *Harvard Business Review*, (November-December 2018).
3 – Owen Edwards, "How the Polaroid Stormed the Photographic World," *Smithsonian Magazine*, (March 2012).
4 – Unnamed Author, presented by the Lemelson-MIT program as part of a series titled "Historical Inventors," www.lemelson.mit.edu.
5 – Ramon Vullings and Marc Meleven, *Not Invented Here*, (BIS Publishing, 2015).
6 – Francesca Gino, "The Business Case for Curiosity," *Harvard Business Review*, (September-October 2018).
7 – Ibid.

Epilogue

1 – Michael Simmons, "Forget 10,000 Hours: Edison, Bezos and Zuckerberg Follow the 10,000-Experiment Rule," *The Observer*, (November 20, 2017).
2 – Barnaby Marsh and Janice Kaplan, Janice. *How Luck Happens*, (Dutton, 2018).
3 – Various authors, "John Sculley," www.wikipedia.com.
4 – Barnaby Marsh and Janice Kaplan, Janice. *How Luck Happens*, (Dutton, 2018).

Praise for Harry's *Get-Real* Message

"Harry's insight, experience and energy are truly inspiring. Our doctors, managers and staff were riveted by his *Get-Real* mindset. He gets to the heart of team culture and what a successful business needs to do to not only survive but thrive in a highly competitive environment for skilled staff and customers. We can't wait to have him back!"

- **Rajesh K. Shetty, M.D. Managing Partner/CEO, Florida Eye Specialists**

"Harry's energy and enthusiasm together with his hands-on real-world experience motivated our members in a very positive way and was a great start to our convention."

- **David Fehling, Executive Director, Association of Diesel Specialists**

"I've had the opportunity to not only listen to Harry deliver dynamic keynote speeches, but to also see the content in action. Harry believes in people, and his encouraging, inspiring style of leadership reflects it. He has an exceptional talent for connecting with and empowering each member of his organization to set the tone for an enjoyable, productive, and successful culture."

- **Courtney Moilanen, Director of Marketing, Durrie Vision**

"'Ridiculously High Energy' is the phrase that come to mind when I think of Harry Campbell. Harry has a fire in his belly for helping others in philanthropic and business pursuits and conveys those messages to his audience from the beginning of his presentation. Harry always left our team wanting more of his powerful and positive message."

> \- **Chandler Cullor EVP, Shareholder, Truss, a Division of HUB International**

"Our associates LOVED Harry Campbell and his *Get-Real* message—so much so they demanded a second and third engagement! And, of course, we obliged their demands because we love that they love his inspirational words on leadership, culture and life. Harry's message is not only real, it is entertaining and a bit raucous (in a good way)! We laughed, cried and learned so much."

> \- **Nancy Whitworth, Chief People Officer, McCownGordon**

"We received rave reviews from our higher education clients about Harry and his *Get-Real* presentation. His content applies to those that are new to leadership, as well as those that have been leaders for many years. Harry's stories and insights are refreshing, engaging, and entertaining."

> \- **Susan McQueeny Scholes, SVP of Marketing, iModules**

"Harry motivated our team of salespeople, across all lines of business, by relating through examples and stories and by breaking down what really matters. No matter what you sell, acknowledge, understand and celebrate your brand."

> \- **Kalinda Calkins, SVP, BOK Financial**

"Harry consistently delivers a highly impactful and motivational presentation. We produce over 30 events around the country each year, and Harry is by far THE BEST keynote speaker I've ever worked with."

> \- **Brian Gargano Regional Director,**
> **Executive Functions Management**

"Harry delivered a memorable, engaging session that brought to life the concepts from his two books, *Get-Real Leadership* and *Get-Real Culture*. Through his own vulnerability, he inspired our leaders to seek 360 feedback and use it to "Get Real" with their own leadership. He invested his time in learning our strategic goals and culture to tailor a session that will help our leaders transform our culture."

> \- **Karen Orosco, SVP US Retail,**
> **H&R Block**

"Harry shared his *Get-Real* experiences with 400 high school seniors from the Northland CAPS (Center for Advanced Professional Studies) program. He held their attention, and all were captivated by his real-world experiences. Harry is an energetic and passionate speaker and a great storyteller."

- **Jon Newcomb, Business Development, Northland CAPS**

"Harry has a remarkable ability to engage and entertain an audience. Drawing you in with compelling stories and lessons from his own corporate and personal life experiences, he delivers relevant and practical advice that is simple to implement within your own organization. If you're looking to re-energize your team or transform your culture, I highly recommend Harry Campbell."

- **Jason Stahl, MD, Owner, Durrie Vision**

"Harry's presentation was engaging, informative and entertaining. His insight on culture and leadership stands out as genuine and pragmatic. I left Harry's presentation ready to take on the world and to be a better leader. Harry has unique experiences that make his presentation approachable for a variety of industries. I would recommend Harry, his presentation and his book to anyone!"

- **Jeff Coppaken, Owner, Coppaken Law Firm**

"Harry is authentic, genuine and a homerun speaker for any organization. He connects with Millennials and Baby Boomers, and from the Boardroom to the Breakroom he is the best when it comes to bringing teams together!"

- **Scott Havens, Vice President, Shareholder at HUB International**

"Harry graciously shared his passion and energy with our optometry students. His enthusiasm was contagious, and his message was well received by our students as they grow towards becoming future professionals."

- **Todd Peabody, OD, MBA, FAAO**
  Associate Dean of Institutional Advancement
  Indiana University School of Optometry

"Harry is majestic on stage and his energy is unstoppable. You'll have 'ah-ha' and 'I've been there' moments as you read his books. Getting real never felt so achievable!"

- **Ashley Mahoney, CEO/Creative Director,**
  Hello Big Idea

"Harry Campbell is a truly engaging speaker with a lifetime of remarkable experience to share. Harry is a master of presenting powerful information with the perfect combination of authority and humility, gravity and humor."

- **Gregg Whittaker, Ph.D.,**
  Former Managing Director and Global
  Head of Credit Derivatives, Chase
  Securities

"Harry has a way of taking complex organizational concepts and explaining them in a simple, actionable way that I can understand and share with my team. His approach is brilliantly simplistic and exactly what is needed in today's business climate."

- **Grant C. Gooding, CEO, PROOF**

"Having experienced the impact of Harry's leadership firsthand in our refractive eye surgery practice, particularly in the realm of office culture, the simple but significant principles he describes carry big weight. The difference between mediocre and excellent businesses is largely the people who make the business go. And Harry understands how to inspire people to be engaged and happy in their workplaces."

- **Timothy Lindquist, MD, Owner, Refractive Surgeon, Durrie Vision**

"Harry brings refreshing candor to all situations in leadership, culture and mindset. He takes the complexity of business and people dynamics into simple and practical applications."

- **Abraham Gin, CEO, Gin Consulting, and Founder, LinkedIn of Local Kansas City**

"It takes a single spark to create a Leadership wildfire. Harry is that spark! His passion, energy, and charisma are unmatched. His direct and pragmatic approach to leadership and team development has benefited thousands. Yet, his desire to connect with people and his willingness to support them in whatever they need is nothing short of inspirational."

- **Matt Reidy, Senior Director, Software Sales Strategy, Cisco Systems**

Also by Harry S. Campbell:

Available on amazon.com

ISBN: 978-1-4679-3552-4

Also by Harry S. Campbell:

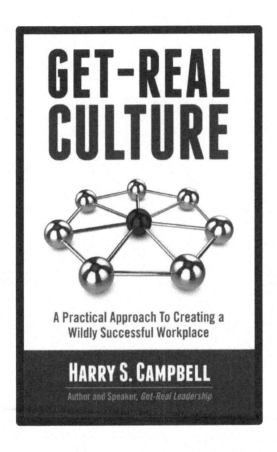

Available on amazon.com

ISBN: 978-1-5328-6348-2